Emergency Contact

Claire McMahon

Professional Reading Series
vanZeno Press
Cleveland, Ohio

ISBN: 978-0-9789244-1-6

Carla Rykowski, Cover Photo
Heidi Della Pesca, Cover Design

For Lena and Ed McMahon

CONTENTS

Above Grief
for my mother,
3/19/36-9/11/2001

No one phoned until,
in a haze mid-morning
you picked up to hear my news.
"I'll walk if I have to,"
Carla from Bleecker,
covered in apartment ashes and
crying
for my mother,
her smoking buddy,
from our basement.

Around the neighborhood
into New York, through
the Holland Tunnel
to Rosie O'Grady's, where
she danced some Saturdays
with my father,
back to Ireland,
her home and her heart,
and on to the New Jersey Italians
Fred di Piazza his
inaudible language--
"An immigrant, like me," my mother said,
who never forgot his homeland or
left it in his head,
not for one moment.

Lena was Irish first,
and loved deeply
particular people she found.
She'd take them in, alter their clothes,
and send them out
styled and suited,
sewing her way into life.

She lighted candles in windows
at Christmas
to welcome the traveler,
"like back home,"
her stories with music
her songs without words
play on in our houses
hymns of comfort,
we can't forget.

Before you go

We know you are still here as
long as you breathe and
you may throw us out anyway, we hope,
to give yourself some peace.

No one moves, just now,
for what seems a long time,
and Brendan and I
watch the rise and fall
of your breaths.

We saw you getting ready,
hesitant at the door;
there's not much left to say.

You may no longer like
hearing the sounds of our living
lullabies and ballads we once knew
"Black is the color of my
true love's hair"

Brendan deaconizes himself
splashing you
with the holy waters of knock.
Later he carries you into Killenagarriff
on his weary shoulder
to your family's resting place,
where you'll meet your own mother
in Irish twilight
under stars just up the road
from the fields
of your young days.

Becoming Religious
for John O'Malley

You talk about NY
and you talk about
meeting me outside
the church on 10th.

Writing in a church,
you say,
is so much more peaceful
than anything else in NY.
What a great idea, I think,
and
it's no problem but,
how do you do
that smoking thing?

Extinguish,
go inside.

The Best of It

Our longings for each other
mount and arrive now
so freely, so fully
like mourning.

At thirty-eight,
we are nearly the same age now,
in what seems like
a sort of
growing up together.

I can't do these things
with you anymore;
you always looking
out the windows
lost in your own head.
Our dark nights
often
filled the house
with heat and desire.

I desire new things now,
as I once desired you

Dear Blog Man

We are rushing away
from the mainframe
can you catch us?
How much money do you need
to write the things you do?
How much freedom
how much joy
what are you doing at your desk
at work behind today's
Plain Dealer web page.

On site,
the elevator breaks down, and we can't
get to you, anyway, if we tried
you'd be tied up
wouldn't you?
Someone down the stairs
has a much deeper voice than they should have
and we wonder
where to put our old wedding rings
so we can get ready
for the action,
one man has recently
told us about.

My Love Is Driving Drunk

My love
is driving drunk
down the road I've left him on
beside the annals of yesterday's plans.

My love
is on the refrain, the rebound;
he stumbles on through traffic
and red light cameras photograph
his darkened license plates.

He moves
only because he is in hiding.

I am not that kind of love.
I am not made up for the occasion.
I am closing all the doors, locking up the house,
tying up my hair and
shaking my head free,
pushing forward
and out
through the embers
of what gets left behind.

My love
is driving drunk
down the road
I've left him on
beside the annals of
yesterday's plans.

Cleaning House

You are leaning too much
to the right
you are leaning on me now,
there's an imaginary lien
on my house
that you left,
where you left things
in the cellar of leanings
toward our lost expectations,

There's just way too much.

I can't hold it all up.

I can't tell you anything.

So
then

The poet calls me up
lets me lean on him
a little while and then
goes away and astray

There's way too much
he says
things to sort through
addresses to change
broken panes in windows
to be fixed.

I can't tell you anything, he says,
you don't already know.

Emergency Contact

When you want to write a poem
it's always an emergency
from tongue to rhythm to tip of pen
you pushed me near the edge
last night at the lake
with your wavering words mapping out
Yeats so sweet
like your mother's memory,
your ramblings
about poetry's found focus
"beyond immortality?"

So many little deaths
we shared
you took me with you,
every time.

First Love Song Memory
for Ed and Grace

Few words
tiny hands,
new baby girl.

I watched you
carry her 'round and 'round
the mountainous
curved hospital corridors passing
concerned midwives and nurses
as you
proudly marched our
Grace,
clutched to your chest.

Is it too late to tell you,
how I watched your every move
then, the two of you,
until you both fell asleep,
like old men in church
in the worn out
vinyl chair
just across from me in the white
bright room.

Our first baby,
cradled like a fox
in blankets
and for the very first time,
asleep,
in her father's arms.

Bar Poetry

The new poet on the scene
was not entirely
remarkable or memorable
in any way
except that it was easy
to tell he was clearly annoyed
with the reactions
to the situations
of his poems
and the noise
of the drunken crowd
in the non-academic bar reading
he was giving
alongside the pool table
while
Iggy Pop's "Raw Power"
wailed out
from the jukebox.

For a Beer

For a beer
I'd give you up
and not realize
I was doing it.

For a beer
I'd drive drunk
to get more beer.

For a beer
I'd blame everything on you
in a made-up fight,
to get to the bar
for a beer.

For a beer
I'd strong arm you
against the doors
you closed
trying to keep me
with you
away from all the beer.

I can't tell you why,
I don't need you;
I'm happy here,
with my beer.

For a beer
I'd restrain you/stop you
from stopping me
on my way to
who knows where
for a beer.

For a beer
I'd damn near
bury you alive
with my addiction
until my lies
drove you damn near mad
for a beer,
I'd promise you all of this.

For a beer
I'd give you up
and never once
look back.

Free, Lemon, Job
for Eileen, my older sister

Under sheets,
side by side
twin beds
I would come visit
warm you up
electric sparks from Nylon legs
under blankets
in darkness
we did the bicycle fast
laughing to movement
heat in winter
a school night
for you
not me
I would go tomorrow
outside alone quiet
make mud pies
wait for you.

Back again to our room
at night
you would quiz me
how to spell
"free" "lemon" "job"
gave me words when I
didn't like to talk
sad in childhood.

16

Lemon was the hardest
the "m" and the "n"
writing
all over concrete
I worked the chalk
through sections of sidewalk
free
lemon
job
a word
a square
avoiding cracks
annoyed with superstition
crayons over
walls of my room
dresser drawers inside
full of free lemon jobs
away from
mother's eye
lemon spelled right
lemon spelled wrong
every night
we practiced,
lights out
for the spelling bee.

For Allen Ginsberg
on the 50th anniversary of "Howl"

Pushing words in wheelbarrows
Down St. Mark's place;
he moves across
this continent of grief
shaking his gray fingers at all of us
quoting Williams and
shouting about men
how indeed they die every day,
for lack of what is found in poetry.

Put out your covert fires,
and find what you'll die for.
Men are dying for the want of knowing.

Ginsberg howls on,
his verse moves
through new generations and
poets looking to be found find Allen
I am grieving, he says,
for my lover for my sons
for my daughters.
I am grieving for lack
of what is found there;
find your poetry
make up for your lack of color
and protest
your dying fathers!
Pay attention
to your falling brothers and sisters!
Sing your own new song.

Growing Up Green
for Bernie Hartigan

When I was little I wanted to be a Green Girl
from Aer Lingus airlines.

I'd dress in all kelly green
with green sheer hose,
green patent leather shoes
matched with dusty green
iridescent eye shadow.

I'd hold real babies
for exhausted, anxious mothers;
babies who threw up
for an entire transcontinental flight
with wet nappies that,
as the Green Girl,
I'd gladly change.

I'd let old men drink too much
powers whiskey,
their small empty bottles
lining the magazine pockets
at the backs of their shamrock-embroidered seats.

It might take a while to be a Green Girl,
I imagined,
but all green and all aglow, at the ready,
and breathless,
my hair tied up in an endless
supply of green ribbons,
I'd move so quickly about the plane
I'd send off streams of green
into the aisles
while adjusting seatbacks.
I'd move into my green zone
where first class passengers
ate Shannon-caught salmon
on royal tara china:
first class
where only the top
Green Girls were allowed to go.

At Shannon,
we'd land and a sea of
Green Girls like me
would whisk through security
and duty free,
planning a mad night's stay
in Dublin, or at the races,
before turning back
to tarmac,
our green beauty
unsurpassed.

Last Christmas

We pulled the damask tablecloth
tightly across the table,
my mother and I.

As she laid it down,
she smoothed out its wrinkles
and pulled down its edges,
just so.

Flowered impressions
gracing our meeting place
like fine bone china,
particularly elegant
without our knowing,
this performance ritual
would be our last.

In the Melon Mitri Room

Lisa and I
sit cross-legged in front of a Buddha
Allen Ginsberg
teaching talking about
how he was in love with
Jack Kerouac and Neal Cassidy
channels William Blake
"oh no! Not again!
Whispers Lisa,
"I think I'm gonna puke,"
but we wait
like obedient disciples
for something to happen
as Allen closes his eyes
tilts his head back and
moves to trace-like mantra
into Blake again.

We hear it now as if for the first time
then onto the
essentials of spontaneous prose
"are you finding you breath?!"
he shouts
in between verses

Not a chance, I'm thinking as my heart
impatiently paces onward and upward
and out from the peaceful practice
Lisa and I try
so desperately to get to
in hopes of graduation,
hand in hand,
from poetry school.

Money Matters

The kitchen is quiet
for once, and
everything falls away.

The worries of mortgage
bills and cups and saucers
have all but
been sorted
in this morning's
light.

We find our own
particular
moments,
as we find
each other, each
morning in the bed beside
the besides of
getting older,
not so much
a place we go;
but a getting
out of it.

New Life in the Development

She is now so newly modern
the chaos of her life sets her off
with her ipod, dvds, & cds all in tow
playing against
her writing
on her laptop,
she says she can't afford this
electric shocks break her back
into city life;
it's clear now she sees,
she's just been
faking it.

And no man now can please her
because all the magic she has once known,
is gone and
impenetrable.

The man she once loved
wants to be remembered for his
penetration only
there wasn't anything memorable
she can remember,
only sounds of
pots and pans; and
hearts closing now
like
excruciating cuts.

The Things You Told Me

The things you told me
arrive sometimes in poetry
you caught up under the sheets
and walking naked through the house.

You are as casual as the air
we push between us.

When I'm not looking
you tidy things I've messed
and pack up the car
like you've done this many times before,
but you haven't.

Always touching my things,
always looking for so long
as if
the troubles can be fixed by looks alone
soft kisses placed where you think I need them
not even all of this helps,
and you know it.

Jodi Singing

Jodi swings
by bass guitar man,
and pouts ever
so sweetly
into microphone.

Our resident boy scout
conga man
comes to her rescue
from behind drums,
fixing wires that pull and record
downloadable versions
of her voice improvisations
long and sometimes low
jazz stories told in ways
I only now
can know.

Because of her,
my poems
read music
that take me beyond
what I know as
standards for
form and content. Jodi goes and she
goes;
and often,
no one
can stop her
when she hits the right note,
and gets us
all swinging.

Poem: "This Is a Poem"
11/9/06

In Canada
you pushed us up against
the tree
and your hands disappeared
inside and
underneath
my vanilla
Irish sweater
sewn
two times over
by the only Italian tailor
I know,
its wool picky enough
to give us both blotches
of this memory.

Your mouth,
drenched in Jameson
whiskey
and tree bark whispered
we wouldn't go undetected,
this time.

Your songs collide now
into my poetry
without Any
particulars, without
intention.

Twilight Walk

And yet,
we have become
so old now
we see one another,
as we are.

Your language
is not new,
but from the ghosts
of Celtic knights
before you.

Your old ways
come back to you,
as I follow you down
through vicious trees full
of our familiar yearning.

I am free now
enough to know you,
standing in twilight's door
as
once before I knew you,
your light's
a heated rhythm,
we longingly explore.

Your Poem Goes On

Your poem goes on
and then it goes
and you go--
you walk out
away from
advice about poetry;
sounds like sounds of certain
hapless wives
who
try their best
to offer up
helpful passion plays
in lieu of
having you leave
to extend yourself
and your dreadful poetry.

Winter Move

Enough!
She screams; he slams doors
behind her
compiling papers and final
pleas for this one last time
addresses the damsel
no longer needed,
no longer waiting,
who hangs up her coat
alone on its hook,
next to her lone hat,
already worn from the early start
of this winter.

Left behind are his piles
of poetry ready for the
pyre, she cooks and
wonders how long
things will take
to burn off,
so that she might see
her way out
amid careful calculations.

The Zen Master Said

The Zen Buddhist master
wrote his sanity statement
on poetics in just under ten minutes:
"I would not consider myself so
much Zen as I would consider
myself a poet of the trees,"
he said.

We weren't so sure what to do
with this oath from druid poser
so we asked
the humming bird, naturally
attracted to the canna shoots
and corpuscles behind us.

Nothing. No luck there.
Just the whir of bird's wings
high on nectar's
found poetry.

Night Visit
for Maeve

Small hands,
touch me
in the night
my daughter
wakes up crying.
We turn on
the light and sit,
turning out
the day's events,
sorting what we've come
to know
and not know.

We bend/we mend
we incline together;
there is no sound,
and our eyes
follow slow shadows
like teardrops
on the wall.

Finely Tuned

He has been mended
on the staircase
he says
finely tuned, ready
and seemingly refreshed
forgiven love
that's forgotten
to finish a job or two
around here.

Later on the bed
he puts himself down,
we curl into mending
and he sleeps as
I watch his lines soften
beside me,
deep into our first
summer's night.

Birthday Poem
for Ed

You took forever to reach me,
a decade and two children.

I tied my boat up
and stood on the dock,
waiting.

Somewhere through this harbor
you followed my light
however faint, however lost
I may have been to you.

Inside me,
you eased flashes
of anger and grief,
leaving
beneath me,
your insurmountable losses.
Your ghosts still wait for you
on that shore:
grief goes on forever
if you let it.
But for today
it won't interrupt us;
we remain
like a boat swinging and clinging
to its dock.

One Chance

He looked at me longer
that day, that night.
It took me out of the play because of it.
There was a delay
in his touch,
a hesitation reserved for
a woman he might be interested in knowing
the palm of his hand
laid on my jacket
just enough in time to rest,
when he spoke, as if
it always had been there.

For Bugsby

My heart
my pocket
your poems
meet me
here
as I am
just now
finished
with analysis
and free to move
without seeing the busy
collaborations made mad
and late at night
we are tired from
the things we pushed,
the things we cannot know.

First Dive

Caroline
center stage
tells jokes
performs charades
in the ocean
fighting waves.
We weave and lean together,
so as not to
go down alone.

Her curls fly
before me through sunlight;
we lock hands
and dive, for the first time,
head first.

Revisions

That poem ends and
off it goes
to the end where
the last lines go
on too long.
Will someone tell *me*?
Frank O'Hara reportedly had no need
or interest in revision
but did he want all those poems found
anyway?
Maybe not.

There's a reason why poets
stuff poems in desk drawers.
If I tell you to eliminate those
last two lines there, will you still sleep
with me? Okay.
Let's wrap our poems like blankets
and hide them from those well-meaning editors.
It's about love and breath, anyway,
our fleeting emotions,
balanced between lips and curves,
take anything you want from this room,
I won't die
without you knowing.

On Writing

So great has
my anxiety become
there is a man in it,

He stands at the crossroads
like Frank O'Hara
awaiting the oncoming traffic
at 3 a.m.

The anxiety inexorably
implodes and
a fairy-
the smallest image-
reaches out
from the paddock
at the very last minute,
and Frank O'Hara lives on
to write so many poems
he builds an entire New York city street;
the skyscrapers, linked
with his words.

Celtic angel,
awash with
poetry and promise
his story turns
fantastic, anxious
and we hitch ourselves to it.

A poet in the darkness
shouts out from his table,
the real story of how
we wait,
with joyful hope,
for something up from purgatory
resembling love and loss,
which makes us live forever,
and brings Frank O'Hara back.

Wrong Hand

For you,
art is seeing.

You speak to me
in hushed
secret tones during lecture hall.

When walking with the poet
you pause
reach out,
walking
beside another poet.
Your brush
sets me off.

Did you see?
I asked—

Yellow dress,
you said --
you and that long hair
smiling.

Yellow dress, smiling
walking with poet,
your hand
in his hand.

On Seeing Things
for Ray

On the playing field,
you pushed me aside so that
on the new dance floor
there was much more room
for us to move.

Later,
John went outside with the Guinness
bottle and a hammer.
When he returned,
the room was quiet
waiting for his story.

He told us of
the brown ale's power
to revive the elderly,
unable to eat in Ireland.

We all nodded knowingly.

But, you, you weren't so sure
about the whole thing,
testing his theory
late into the night.
Later we talked about
past loves and children.

I sent you off stumbling
to the youngest woman available.

In morning's light,
we were sorted;
quietly we ate our tea and toast.

42

Mulling

I've not much poetry left
to call you names in.
Days go by too quick
and I'm wondering when
grief will hit.
When you're not looking,
a friend assures me.

Anyway, there's more room here
to plant and grow
out the things
that have taken
so long to collapse.

I don't need
the restraint of your
strong-armed love
or even
to lock up the house,
the night has just
become itself; dark
and sometimes full with
harvest moon
and swallows love.

You stopped walking with me
in it
ages ago.

Blue Haiku

Blue dog sits up;
baby Anna holds his hand
fine art of teaching.

Porch Song
Boulder, Colorado

The sun
doesn't shine
close enough near enough,
the front
of the house
is shaded so I go out
a few steps
to the sidewalk.

The new kitten
sprung from
boulder's humane society jail
$45 bail

Runs after ants
jumps at my pen
rolls in dirt.

The sun (that always shines here)
feels good all over
my freckles
I keep my face down
toward paper,
so they do not multiply.

Neighborhood News

The air seems
never clear here
the fights go on for days
and rise up
out of storms that turn into
ebbing years.

Outside
all seems ordinary,
and the folks put decorations up
for the seasons;
a hired boy
cuts the lawn
that no longer belongs to anyone.

He works for himself
wanting to be the boy alone.
His hears nothing underneath ipod
and locomotive whisper
of lawn mower.

Everything is as it was
just yesterday.

My Sister Has a Theory

That a man
can only serve
one woman. So,
if his mother is alive and
he decides on marriage
the struggle
for wherefore
he may put
his passions
for attention
will invoke
new complications and
new rules for servitude.

The man can, indeed,
he might admit,
only serve one woman,
and if he does one well
he will remain with that
particular woman
for a time.

She will be his lover,
she will be his mother;
she will be enough.

Love and Food

There was something
about eating
I didn't like at first;
maybe it was the flavor of your skin.

I didn't like meat,
I didn't like vegetables,
it took some power away
from the tables
we sat at
foods taking matters of love
and obsession
to new possibilities
of consumption.

There was something
about eating
with you,
I didn't like.

The Cape Cod Collaborations

Orion and Marguerite
are lovers now;
used to be
Orion'd hit on me
dropping his bottles
in the middle of a poet
while talking to me.

Then
he left with Marguerite,
the educated, well-housed poet
for Cape Cod.

There they were lovers
and wrote what were said to be
horrible collaborations and
long devoted collections
of notes on
unlikely love.

From New York today,
Maryann writes to tell me he's back
and clanking bottles
at every poet in town.

He reads, in familiar Russian accent, his
"Cape Cod Collaborations"
with heat with fervor
with mentions
of deceit, but we know
from knowing,
how it all crashed down.

Happily Married

The sheets
damp with alcohol fumes
and lies
touch me only slightly
tonight and for once
I do not feel sorry
for my choices.

A part of me
is stuck here
in the business of life
and money.

I am not talking anymore.
I am not writing anymore.
I am staying on task.

I collect wood, raise children,
flip through the manuscripts.
All efforts to keep connections
Between the imagined and the real.

For Kevin

My injured brother,
on maneuvers
prepping for panama
in dark Kentucky night's
training ground.
The captain asked:
"you want a souvenir, maam?"
I turned the gold shell in my hand
imagining its explosion inside my brother
entering his abdomen from 20 yards away.
Underfoot, bullets crunched and rolled
mixed with broken chem lights and dust,
and uneven, sand-like traps
poised over
man-made hills .

The Rangers of
Fort Campbell greeted us
with bowed heads
and news of my brother,
Army Sgt. First Class,
Airborne Ranger.

We sat and waited for weeks
and Brendan slept by your side
knocking an occasional hospital cart over
and pounding desks
demanding shots of morphine. When your eyes opened
that August day,
the war was won,
our mother said.
After ten long years,
you had put down your gun.

For Kitty

Today borders on the real;
the end of an agreement--
you did agree, didn't you?

The papers will itemize
your life in partitions;
present parcels of land deeds
and previous owners.

You have not been owned.
You have wanted some things.

No one hears you
speaking anymore.
As small as you are, your voice grows slowly weaker
but still, you settle to agree
without wanting
without knowing

What you were planning for.

Distance

I liked that
you never knew
the appropriate sense of space
or pretended to anyway
banging your bony hip
against mine
what were you up to
in the bookstore
and behind the glass
at the Book of Kells display
that you insisted
I should not go to.
You acted as my guide, anyway

I thought we were cousins
you proved
we were not
as you looked through me,
with your western Irish-blue eyes
glassy from mid-afternoon drinks.

Standing at the Arch of Trinity
you had become a man
filled out in the shoulders,
muscular in the legs, not the you
I knew but still the same slow tongue
you slowed me right down-
"This is not New York," you said
leaning me on the campus wall,

Our secret space exposed.

Moving
for Frank O'Hara and Bill Berkson

I've been moved before.
Lately I moved house.
You didn't help. I watched you move across the stage
moving hips and spine like you knew I was watching.
I see it in the moves you make
when you write poetry.
You are conscious of making moves in your line
    arrangements
like Frank O'Hara in "Biotherm"- - a marvelous
sunburn beauty cream owned by Bill Berkson's mother.

Frank O'Hara made moves on Bill Berkson until
his untimely death in 1966,
his moves never to be forgotten.
Move out of my way, Frank,
there's a poem here,
can you see it?

Bill moves me
to the front of the lecture hall
he pulls the chiffon at the back of my dress
that is yellow.

That's his voice.
That's his line there.I move with him across the campus
sometimes so much
linked that we move together.
Bill is conscious of making moves,
he moves many women
and parts blue-eyed seas; mostly,
he moves me.

Poetry Lesson/Kitchen
with Grace and Maeve

What could that poet mean?
In her deepest poetic voice she
cites:
"and I didn't want Any deviled eggs?"
Mommy, *can you help me?*
Well. The poet was obviously
not very hungry. She raises her eyebrow.
"or sad," she says. "too sad to eat, maybe?"
only the poet knows.
But why is it there
if we can't know?
It's like a secret, I explain.
Like a *dumb* secret, she sends back.
No, deviled eggs are for happy times, I say.
Like a picnic? She asks.
Exactly.
But he didn't want Any, mommy.
Yes, the poor poet.
He is very sad.
Maybe he is dying.

Poetry Workshop
for Anselm Hollo & Grace

Make a poem
make a craft
put the image
square between us-
more metaphor! More simile!
You can't explain
without comparing it
abstraction in poetry is where it's at
deviled eggs found everywhere-
remarkable! You say
and laugh in the kitchen
at us back to back,
in the imaginary kitchen
on our imaginary chairs.

"More Than the Ear Can Hold"
(after Frank O'Hara)

She studied the mirror
to view herself on tiptoes
pointed and swaying to
a "rock" as they call it
in her version of American-Irish
dance
the steps differ
from place to place
teacher to teacher
new dances invented
on the heels of Mr.
Michael Flatley
she studies her feet and
makes her own new steps
counting softly the music
times it for the ear
"help me with the *start* of it"
she whispers
hesitantly—

"Go on with yerself , girl!" He yells to
takes her out of it and
she hops up
to compete
legs in thighs,
ear
to music.

Today's Tea

Today
drank tea at least
six hours straight
Kitty has her kettle
on boiling constant
always ready for me
Irish tea bag in place
the commercial we talk about
is effective we think
it lightens itself through poetry,
but not exactly,
we decide over the tea.

What is it I wanted here?
To hear your story of the day
and your losses
still occurring
keep your waters going, Kitty
"he may not be back"
turns into, "why
you can't wait."

What Time Is It in Ireland?

What time is it in Ireland?

We often asked you this,
our Irish-American question.

Immediately, you'd look up
at the tiled kitchen clock
and tell us what might be happening
over there.

Your answer was not about the time
but the event of the day.

Maybe your brother Jimmy
was sitting down to a full plate of sausages now
after the milking-
the cast iron skillet
placed directly on the farm table
to serve himself
a "fine feed", as he would say.

Or later,
we'd imagine him asleep in the loft
with an ear out for
a calving cow.

He was responsible man,
and often stared out the window
at the field
she was housed in.

When we weren't in Ireland,
we missed it.
We missed the hayloft
with Jimmy's homemade tire swing,
the Collins' shop at the end of the bohereen
full of Cadbury's dairy milkbars
of golden ticketed heaven.

We missed too the sounds and
click clack of cow hooves
outside our windows at sunrise.
We knew then it was milking time.

It wasn't work to us - *the Yanks* -
home again in summer.

We lived our lives on Irish time
counting days left before the
start of school in America,
we split our lives between the seas,
back home again with mother;
the island she never left.

Virus

I am trying desperately
to read between your lines.

Is the disk full of virus
for any particular reason?
The words jump and twist like maggots
on the page
oops! There goes one now
over and beyond
the paragraph revised
to include something about where
I found you talking in
mid-conversation.

Calling up the webmaster
I promised flowers, drinks
to fix you properly
I watched your words move out
I watched you drink too much and
slam the car into trees in the driveway
is alcoholism a virus
I just can't sort out?

What happened to the morning
with you in it
what happened to the conversation
the paragraph revised
has it all gone missing like our dead lovers?
The front of the disk reads: "Frank"
and Maeve holds it
with regard
"is this the bugged one?" She asks,
fingering it
as if
she might catch it.

To Breast Cancer

In the name of my mother,
I write you this poem.
You, breast cancer, standing in the shower
beside the woman,
washing herself
and finding her first lump.

In the name of my mother,
my sister, my brothers,
my girlfriends,
I write you this poem,
breast cancer,
and I command you
to get out.

You were not invited
to this life's party,
attacking women where
they are most vulnerable;
where they are honored in history
with sculptures of beauty:
the breast.

Straight against these lights,
I look at the cancers
that don't show up on mammograms
that they tell us are "a process"
that have been growing
inside us
for years and years
as if
it is now our fault.
A disease of confusion, of rejection,
of self-actualization.

My husband never touched me
the same way again, she said
when my breasts
were taken.

Breast cancer,
you've got a lot of nerve
invading our love lives
and scaring our men
as if they weren't scared enough already!

How dare you
take up the lives
and time of mothers,
who walk themselves to radiation
and chemotherapy to "get the air"
as they worry
they won't get enough of it.

Breast-cancered women joke through
their worries pushing
themselves through the disease until
they hear the words
"cancer free" from doctors
and they do not draw
a sigh of relief
even then,
as you wait like a stalker, you coward.
Breast cancer,
I command your numbered
proportions
to stop growing
to stop taking
all our beauty
the art
we all have come to know
as women
and their necessary places
in our lives
how dare you
come invading, uninvited
to our mothers, our sisters, our friends

how dare you.

Sundays at Gaelic Park
for Dad

I remember you
in boxer shorts
curling hurling sticks
black eyes and
foul mouth running
on that worn-down,
brown Bronx field.

We sat on wood-ply benches
screaming out county names found
in all parts of Ireland,
Mary Riordan often
leading the chant,
passing fistfuls of money
back to all the lads
for ice cream occupations
and visits to the on-site pub.

You were the MVP hurler
and could balance
that ball
on a stick
at least 50 yards before blasting it
into its home place,
sometimes taking some skin
off the goalie
on its way.

No fear,
no bother,
plenty of fair play.

vanZeno Press

www.vanzenopress.com

Our concept is to publish fine books of poetry and allow poets to be the retail and distribution system themselves. Who do we publish? Poets who are serious about their work, who actively read at poetry readings and other events, poets our editorial board believes meet our standards of excellence, and deserve to be published.

Our poets are paid a royalty for every book sold by vanZeno Press or by Amazon, Borders, or whoever. Our books have a vanZeno Press ISBN number and are listed in Books In Print. What makes vanZeno different from other publishing companies is the way we try to get the poet to make the most money. The poet, by reading out in local venues, makes the biggest profit on his or her book: the difference between the price he or she sells it for, and the very reasonable cost of the book from vanZeno Press.

This puts the money where it belongs: in the poet's pocket. Nobody is likely to get rich, but we think it will at the least pay for gas and lunch or dinner at the reading gigs. If you're interested in submitting a manuscript or in learning more about our publishing process, please email us at editor@vanzenopress.com.